BE

brave, strong, courageous

& KIND

Seek adventure

TRUTH AND LOVE

Download the FREE

"30 Days of Affirmations for Positive and Healthy Living Journal"

When you sign up at

www.arianaplanner.com

Use this FREE download as a:

- Companion to this planner. Start each day with one affirmation and plan your day ahead with more clarity and focus.
- Standalone gratitude journal

---

plannersariana

admin@arianaplanner.com

Ariana Planner

Personal Profile

Name: ______________________________
Address: ______________________________
____
Phone: ______________________________
E-mail: ______________________________

Businesss

Name: ______________________________
Address: ______________________________
____
Phone: ______________________________
E-mail: ______________________________

Emergency Contacts

Name: ______________________________
Phone: ______________________________
E-mail: ______________________________

Name: ______________________________
Phone: ______________________________
E-mail: ______________________________

Name: ______________________________
Phone: ______________________________
E-mail: ______________________________

Name: ______________________________
Phone: ______________________________
E-mail: ______________________________

Doctor's Name: ______________________________
Phone: ______________________________
E-mail: ______________________________

Doctor's Name: ______________________________
Phone: ______________________________
E-mail: ______________________________

Police: ______________________________
Phone: ______________________________
E-mail: ______________________________

Fire: ______________________________
Phone: ______________________________
E-mail: ______________________________

Other

____
____
____
____
____
____

Contact Names	Contact Names
Name: ______ Phone: ______ E-mail: ______	Name: ______ Phone: ______ E-mail: ______
Name: ______ Phone: ______ E-mail: ______	Name: ______ Phone: ______ E-mail: ______
Name: ______ Phone: ______ E-mail: ______	Name: ______ Phone: ______ E-mail: ______
Name: ______ Phone: ______ E-mail: ______	Name: ______ Phone: ______ E-mail: ______
Name: ______ Phone: ______ E-mail: ______	Name: ______ Phone: ______ E-mail: ______
Name: ______ Phone: ______ E-mail: ______	Name: ______ Phone: ______ E-mail: ______
Name: ______ Phone: ______ E-mail: ______	Name: ______ Phone: ______ E-mail: ______

Password Log

Website: ____________________
Username: ____________________
Password: ____________________
Notes: ____________________

Website: ____________________
Username: ____________________
Password: ____________________
Notes: ____________________

Website: ____________________
Username: ____________________
Password: ____________________
Notes: ____________________

Website: ____________________
Username: ____________________
Password: ____________________
Notes: ____________________

Website: ____________________
Username: ____________________
Password: ____________________
Notes: ____________________

Website: ____________________
Username: ____________________
Password: ____________________
Notes: ____________________

Website: ____________________
Username: ____________________
Password: ____________________
Notes: ____________________

Website: ____________________
Username: ____________________
Password: ____________________
Notes: ____________________

Website: ____________________
Username: ____________________
Password: ____________________
Notes: ____________________

Website: ____________________
Username: ____________________
Password: ____________________
Notes: ____________________

Password Log

Website:
Username:
Password:
Notes:

Website:
Username:
Password:
Notes:

Website:
Username:
Password:
Notes:

Website:
Username:
Password:
Notes:

Website:
Username:
Password:
Notes:

Website:
Username:
Password:
Notes:

Website:
Username:
Password:
Notes:

Website:
Username:
Password:
Notes:

Website:
Username:
Password:
Notes:

Website:
Username:
Password:
Notes:

Birthday Log

January

February

March

April

May

June

July

August

September

October

November

December

2022

January

S	M	T	W	T	F	S
30	31					1
2	3	4	5	6	7	8
9	10	11	12	13	14	15
16	17	18	19	20	21	22
23	24	25	26	27	28	29

February

S	M	T	W	T	F	S
		1	2	3	4	5
6	7	8	9	10	11	12
13	14	15	16	17	18	19
20	21	22	23	24	25	26
27	28					

March

S	M	T	W	T	F	S
		1	2	3	4	5
6	7	8	9	10	11	12
13	14	15	16	17	18	19
20	21	22	23	24	25	26
27	28	29	30	31		

April

S	M	T	W	T	F	S
					1	2
3	4	5	6	7	8	9
10	11	12	13	14	15	16
17	18	19	20	21	22	23
24	25	26	27	28	29	30

May

S	M	T	W	T	F	S
1	2	3	4	5	6	7
8	9	10	11	12	13	14
15	16	17	18	19	20	21
22	23	24	25	26	27	28
29	30	31				

June

S	M	T	W	T	F	S
			1	2	3	4
5	6	7	8	9	10	11
12	13	14	15	16	17	18
19	20	21	22	23	24	25
26	27	28	29	30		

IMPORTANT DATES

2022

July

S	M	T	W	T	F	S
31					1	2
3	4	5	6	7	8	9
10	11	12	13	14	15	16
17	18	19	20	21	22	23
24	25	26	27	28	29	30

August

S	M	T	W	T	F	S
	1	2	3	4	5	6
7	8	9	10	11	12	13
14	15	16	17	18	19	20
21	22	23	24	25	26	27
28	29	30	31			

September

S	M	T	W	T	F	S
				1	2	3
4	5	6	7	8	9	10
11	12	13	14	15	16	17
18	19	20	21	22	23	24
25	26	27	28	29	30	

October

S	M	T	W	T	F	S
30	31					1
2	3	4	5	6	7	8
9	10	11	12	13	14	15
16	17	18	19	20	21	22
23	24	25	26	27	28	29

November

S	M	T	W	T	F	S
		1	2	3	4	5
6	7	8	9	10	11	12
13	14	15	16	17	18	19
20	21	22	23	24	25	26
27	28	29	30			

December

S	M	T	W	T	F	S
				1	2	3
4	5	6	7	8	9	10
11	12	13	14	15	16	17
18	19	20	21	22	23	24
25	26	27	28	29	30	31

IMPORTANT DATES

January 2022

SUNDAY	MONDAY	TUESDAY	WEDNESDAY
2	3	4	5
9	10	11	12
16	17 Martin Luther King Day	18	19
23 / 30	24 / 31	25	26

THURSDAY	FRIDAY	SATURDAY
		1 New Year's Day
6	7	8
13	14	15
20	21	22
27	28	29

NOTES

February 2022

SUNDAY	MONDAY	TUESDAY	WEDNESDAY
		1	2
6	7	8	9
13	14 Valentine's Day	15	16
20	21 President's Day	22	23
27	28		

THURSDAY	FRIDAY	SATURDAY
3	4	5
10	11	12
17	18	19
24	25	26

NOTES

March 2022

SUNDAY	MONDAY	TUESDAY	WEDNESDAY
		1	2
6	7	8	9
13	14	15	16
20	21	22	23
27	28	29	30

THURSDAY	FRIDAY	SATURDAY
3	4	5
10	11	12
17 St. Patrick's Day	18	19
24	25	26
31		

NOTES

April 2022

SUNDAY	MONDAY	TUESDAY	WEDNESDAY
3	4	5	6
10	11	12	13
17 Easter	18	19	20
24	25	26	27

THURSDAY	FRIDAY	SATURDAY
	1	2
7	8	9
14	15 Good Friday	16
21	22	23
28	29	30

NOTES

May 2022

SUNDAY	MONDAY	TUESDAY	WEDNESDAY
1	2	3	4
8 Mother's Day	9	10	11
15	16	17	18
22	23	24	25
29	30 Memorial Day	31	

THURSDAY	FRIDAY	SATURDAY
5	6	7
12	13	14
19	20	21
26	27	28

NOTES

June 2022

SUNDAY	MONDAY	TUESDAY	WEDNESDAY
			1
5	6	7	8
12	13	14	15
19 Father's Day	20	21	22
26	27	28	29

THURSDAY	FRIDAY	SATURDAY
2	3	4
9	10	11
16	17	18
23	24	25
30		

NOTES

July 2022

SUNDAY	MONDAY	TUESDAY	WEDNESDAY
3	4 Independence Day	5	6
10	11	12	13
17	18	19	20
24 / 31	25	26	27

THURSDAY	FRIDAY	SATURDAY
	1	2
7	8	9
14	15	16
21	22	23
28	29	30

NOTES

August 2022

SUNDAY	MONDAY	TUESDAY	WEDNESDAY
	1	2	3
7	8	9	10
14	15	16	17
21	22	23	24
28	29	30	31

THURSDAY	FRIDAY	SATURDAY
4	5	6
11	12	13
18	19	20
25	26	27

NOTES

September 2022

SUNDAY	MONDAY	TUESDAY	WEDNESDAY
4	5 Labor Day	6	7
11	12	13	14
18	19	20	21
25	26	27	28

THURSDAY	FRIDAY	SATURDAY
1	2	3
8	9	10
15	16	17
22	23	24
29	30	

NOTES

October 2022

SUNDAY	MONDAY	TUESDAY	WEDNESDAY
2	3	4	5
9	10 Columbus Day	11	12
16	17	18	19
23 / 30	24 / 31 Halloween	25	26

THURSDAY	FRIDAY	SATURDAY
		1
6	7	8
13	14	15
20	21	22
27	28	29

NOTES

November 2022

SUNDAY	MONDAY	TUESDAY	WEDNESDAY
		1	2
6	7	8	9
13	14	15	16
20	21	22	23
27	28	29	30

THURSDAY	FRIDAY	SATURDAY
3	4	5
10	11 Veterans Day	12
17	18	19
24 Thanksgiving Day	25	26

NOTES

December 2022

SUNDAY	MONDAY	TUESDAY	WEDNESDAY
4	5	6	7
11	12	13	14
18	19	20	21
25 Christmas	26	27	28

THURSDAY	FRIDAY	SATURDAY
1	2	3
8	9	10
15	16	17
22	23	24
29	30	31

NOTES

2023

January

S	M	T	W	T	F	S
1	2	3	4	5	6	7
8	9	10	11	12	13	14
15	16	17	18	19	20	21
22	23	24	25	26	27	28
29	30	31				

February

S	M	T	W	T	F	S
			1	2	3	4
5	6	7	8	9	10	11
12	13	14	15	16	17	18
19	20	21	22	23	24	25
26	27	28				

March

S	M	T	W	T	F	S
			1	2	3	4
5	6	7	8	9	10	11
12	13	14	15	16	17	18
19	20	21	22	23	24	25
26	27	28	29	30	31	

April

S	M	T	W	T	F	S
30						1
2	3	4	5	6	7	8
9	10	11	12	13	14	15
16	17	18	19	20	21	22
23	24	25	26	27	28	29

May

S	M	T	W	T	F	S
	1	2	3	4	5	6
7	8	9	10	11	12	13
14	15	16	17	18	19	20
21	22	23	24	25	26	27
28	29	30	31			

June

S	M	T	W	T	F	S
				1	2	3
4	5	6	7	8	9	10
11	12	13	14	15	16	17
18	19	20	21	22	23	24
25	26	27	28	29	30	

IMPORTANT DATES

2023

July

S	M	T	W	T	F	S
30	31					1
2	3	4	5	6	7	8
9	10	11	12	13	14	15
16	17	18	19	20	21	22
23	24	25	26	27	28	29

August

S	M	T	W	T	F	S
		1	2	3	4	5
6	7	8	9	10	11	12
13	14	15	16	17	18	19
20	21	22	23	24	25	26
27	28	29	30	31		

September

S	M	T	W	T	F	S
					1	2
3	4	5	6	7	8	9
10	11	12	13	14	15	16
17	18	19	20	21	22	23
24	25	26	27	28	29	30

October

S	M	T	W	T	F	S
1	2	3	4	5	6	7
8	9	10	11	12	13	14
15	16	17	18	19	20	21
22	23	24	25	26	27	28
29	30	31				

November

S	M	T	W	T	F	S
			1	2	3	4
5	6	7	8	9	10	11
12	13	14	15	16	17	18
19	20	21	22	23	24	25
26	27	28	29	30		

December

S	M	T	W	T	F	S
31					1	2
3	4	5	6	7	8	9
10	11	12	13	14	15	16
17	18	19	20	21	22	23
24	25	26	27	28	29	30

IMPORTANT DATES

January 2023

SUNDAY	MONDAY	TUESDAY	WEDNESDAY
1 New Year's Day	2	3	4
8	9	10	11
15	16 Martin Luther King Day	17	18
22	23	24	25
29	30	31	

THURSDAY	FRIDAY	SATURDAY
5	6	7
12	13	14
19	20	21
26	27	28

NOTES

February 2023

SUNDAY	MONDAY	TUESDAY	WEDNESDAY
			1
5	6	7	8
12	13	14 Valentine's Day	15
19	20 President's Day	21	22
26	27	28	

THURSDAY	FRIDAY	SATURDAY
2	3	4
9	10	11
16	17	18
23	24	25

NOTES

March 2023

SUNDAY	MONDAY	TUESDAY	WEDNESDAY
			1
5	6	7	8
12	13	14	15
19	20	21	22
26	27	28	29

THURSDAY	FRIDAY	SATURDAY
2	3	4
9	10	11
16	17 St. Patrick's Day	18
23	24	25
30	31	

NOTES

April 2023

SUNDAY	MONDAY	TUESDAY	WEDNESDAY
2	3	4	5
9 Easter	10	11	12
16	17	18	19
23 / 30	24	25	26

THURSDAY	FRIDAY	SATURDAY
		1
6	7 Good Friday	8
13	14	15
20	21	22
27	28	29

NOTES

May 2023

SUNDAY	MONDAY	TUESDAY	WEDNESDAY
	1	2	3
7	8	9	10
14 Mother's Day	15	16	17
21	22	23	24
28	29 Memorial Day	30	31

THURSDAY	FRIDAY	SATURDAY
4	5	6
11	12	13
18	19	20
25	26	27

NOTES

June 2023

SUNDAY	MONDAY	TUESDAY	WEDNESDAY
4	5	6	7
11	12	13	14
18 Father's Day	19	20	21
25	26	27	28

THURSDAY	FRIDAY	SATURDAY
1	2	3
8	9	10
15	16	17
22	23	24
29	30	

NOTES

July 2023

SUNDAY	MONDAY	TUESDAY	WEDNESDAY
2	3	4 Independence Day	5
9	10	11	12
16	17	18	19
23 / 30	24 / 31	25	26

THURSDAY	FRIDAY	SATURDAY
		1
6	7	8
13	14	15
20	21	22
27	28	29

NOTES

August 2023

SUNDAY	MONDAY	TUESDAY	WEDNESDAY
		1	2
6	7	8	9
13	14	15	16
20	21	22	23
27	28	29	30

THURSDAY	FRIDAY	SATURDAY
3	4	5
10	11	12
17	18	19
24	25	26
31		

NOTES

September 2023

SUNDAY	MONDAY	TUESDAY	WEDNESDAY
3	4 Labor Day	5	6
10	11	12	13
17	18	19	20
24	25	26	27

THURSDAY	FRIDAY	SATURDAY
	1	2
7	8	9
14	15	16
21	22	23
28	29	30

NOTES

October 2023

SUNDAY	MONDAY	TUESDAY	WEDNESDAY
1	2	3	4
8	9 Columbus Day	10	11
15	16	17	18
22	23	24	25
29	30	31 Halloween	

THURSDAY	FRIDAY	SATURDAY
5	6	7
12	13	14
19	20	21
26	27	28

NOTES

November 2023

SUNDAY	MONDAY	TUESDAY	WEDNESDAY
			1
5	6	7	8
12	13	14	15
19	20	21	22
26	27	28	29

THURSDAY	FRIDAY	SATURDAY
2	3	4
9	10	11 Veterans Day
16	17	18
23 Thanksgiving Day	24	25
30		

NOTES

December 2023

SUNDAY	MONDAY	TUESDAY	WEDNESDAY
3	4	5	6
10	11	12	13
17	18	19	20
24 / 31	25 Christmas	26	27

THURSDAY	FRIDAY	SATURDAY
	1	2
7	8	9
14	15	16
21	22	23
28	29	30

NOTES

2024

January

S	M	T	W	T	F	S
	1	2	3	4	5	6
7	8	9	10	11	12	13
14	15	16	17	18	19	20
21	22	23	24	25	26	27
28	29	30	31			

February

S	M	T	W	T	F	S
				1	2	3
4	5	6	7	8	9	10
11	12	13	14	15	16	17
18	19	20	21	22	23	24
25	26	27	28	29		

March

S	M	T	W	T	F	S
31					1	2
3	4	5	6	7	8	9
10	11	12	13	14	15	16
17	18	19	20	21	22	23
24	25	26	27	28	29	30

April

S	M	T	W	T	F	S
	1	2	3	4	5	6
7	8	9	10	11	12	13
14	15	16	17	18	19	20
21	22	23	24	25	26	27
28	29	30				

May

S	M	T	W	T	F	S
			1	2	3	4
5	6	7	8	9	10	11
12	13	14	15	16	17	18
19	20	21	22	23	24	25
26	27	28	29	30	31	

June

S	M	T	W	T	F	S
30						1
2	3	4	5	6	7	8
9	10	11	12	13	14	15
16	17	18	19	20	21	22
23	24	25	26	27	28	29

IMPORTANT DATES

2024

July

S	M	T	W	T	F	S
	1	2	3	4	5	6
7	8	9	10	11	12	13
14	15	16	17	18	19	20
21	22	23	24	25	26	27
28	29	30	31			

August

S	M	T	W	T	F	S
				1	2	3
4	5	6	7	8	9	10
11	12	13	14	15	16	17
18	19	20	21	22	23	24
25	26	27	28	29	30	31

September

S	M	T	W	T	F	S
1	2	3	4	5	6	7
8	9	10	11	12	13	14
15	16	17	18	19	20	21
22	23	24	25	26	27	28
29	30					

October

S	M	T	W	T	F	S
		1	2	3	4	5
6	7	8	9	10	11	12
13	14	15	16	17	18	19
20	21	22	23	24	25	26
27	28	29	30	31		

November

S	M	T	W	T	F	S
					1	2
3	4	5	6	7	8	9
10	11	12	13	14	15	16
17	18	19	20	21	22	23
24	25	26	27	28	29	30

December

S	M	T	W	T	F	S
1	2	3	4	5	6	7
8	9	10	11	12	13	14
15	16	17	18	19	20	21
22	23	24	25	26	27	28
29	30	31				

IMPORTANT DATES

January 2024

SUNDAY	MONDAY	TUESDAY	WEDNESDAY
	1 New Year's Day	2	3
7	8	9	10
14	15 Martin Luther King Day	16	17
21	22	23	24
28	29	30	31

THURSDAY	FRIDAY	SATURDAY
4	5	6
11	12	13
18	19	20
25	26	27

NOTES

February 2024

SUNDAY	MONDAY	TUESDAY	WEDNESDAY
4	5	6	7
11	12	13	14 Valentine's Day
18	19 President's Day	20	21
25	26	27	28

THURSDAY	FRIDAY	SATURDAY
1	2	3
8	9	10
15	16	17
22	23	24
29		

NOTES

March 2024

SUNDAY	MONDAY	TUESDAY	WEDNESDAY
3	4	5	6
10	11	12	13
17 St. Patrick's Day	18	19	20
24 / 31 Easter	25	26	27

THURSDAY	FRIDAY	SATURDAY
	1	2
7	8	9
14	15	16
21	22	23
28	29 Good Friday	30

NOTES

April 2024

SUNDAY	MONDAY	TUESDAY	WEDNESDAY
	1	2	3
7	8	9	10
14	15	16	17
21	22	23	24
28	29	30	

THURSDAY	FRIDAY	SATURDAY
4	5	6
11	12	13
18	19	20
25	26	27

NOTES

May 2024

SUNDAY	MONDAY	TUESDAY	WEDNESDAY
			1
5	6	7	8
12 Mother's Day	13	14	15
19	20	21	22
26	27 Memorial Day	28	29

THURSDAY	FRIDAY	SATURDAY
2	3	4
9	10	11
16	17	18
23	24	25
30	31	

NOTES

June 2024

SUNDAY	MONDAY	TUESDAY	WEDNESDAY
2	3	4	5
9	10	11	12
16 Father's Day	17	18	19
23 / 30	24	25	26

THURSDAY	FRIDAY	SATURDAY
		1
6	7	8
13	14	15
20	21	22
27	28	29

NOTES

July 2024

SUNDAY	MONDAY	TUESDAY	WEDNESDAY
	1	2	3
7	8	9	10
14	15	16	17
21	22	23	24
28	29	30	31

THURSDAY	FRIDAY	SATURDAY
4 Independence Day	5	6
11	12	13
18	19	20
25	26	27

NOTES

August 2024

SUNDAY	MONDAY	TUESDAY	WEDNESDAY
4	5	6	7
11	12	13	14
18	19	20	21
25	26	27	28

THURSDAY	FRIDAY	SATURDAY
1	2	3
8	9	10
15	16	17
22	23	24
29	30	31

NOTES

September 2024

SUNDAY	MONDAY	TUESDAY	WEDNESDAY
1	2 Labor Day	3	4
8	9	10	11
15	16	17	18
22	23	24	25
29	30		

THURSDAY	FRIDAY	SATURDAY
5	6	7
12	13	14
19	20	21
26	27	28

NOTES

October 2024

SUNDAY	MONDAY	TUESDAY	WEDNESDAY
		1	2
6	7	8	9
13	14 Columbus Day	15	16
20	21	22	23
27	28	29	30

THURSDAY	FRIDAY	SATURDAY
3	4	5
10	11	12
17	18	19
24	25	26
31 Halloween		

NOTES

November 2024

SUNDAY	MONDAY	TUESDAY	WEDNESDAY
3	4	5	6
10	11 Veterans Day	12	13
17	18	19	20
24	25	26	27

THURSDAY	FRIDAY	SATURDAY
	1	2
7	8	9
14	15	16
21	22	23
28 Thanksgiving Day	29	30

NOTES

December 2024

SUNDAY	MONDAY	TUESDAY	WEDNESDAY
1	2	3	4
8	9	10	11
15	16	17	18
22	23	24	25 Christmas
29	30	31	

THURSDAY	FRIDAY	SATURDAY
5	6	7
12	13	14
19	20	21
26	27	28

NOTES

2025

January

S	M	T	W	T	F	S
			1	2	3	4
5	6	7	8	9	10	11
12	13	14	15	16	17	18
19	20	21	22	23	24	25
26	27	28	29	30	31	

February

S	M	T	W	T	F	S
						1
2	3	4	5	6	7	8
9	10	11	12	13	14	15
16	17	18	19	20	21	22
23	24	25	26	27	28	

March

S	M	T	W	T	F	S
30	31					1
2	3	4	5	6	7	8
9	10	11	12	13	14	15
16	17	18	19	20	21	22
23	24	25	26	27	28	29

April

		1	2	3	4	5
6	7	8	9	10	11	12
13	14	15	16	17	18	19
20	21	22	23	24	25	26
27	28	29	30			

May

				1	2	3
4	5	6	7	8	9	10
11	12	13	14	15	16	17
18	19	20	21	22	23	24
25	26	27	28	29	30	31

June

1	2	3	4	5	6	7
8	9	10	11	12	13	14
15	16	17	18	19	20	21
22	23	24	25	26	27	28
29	30					

IMPORTANT DATES

2025

July

S	M	T	W	T	F	S
		1	2	3	4	5
6	7	8	9	10	11	12
13	14	15	16	17	18	19
20	21	22	23	24	25	26
27	28	29	30	31		

August

S	M	T	W	T	F	S
31					1	2
3	4	5	6	7	8	9
10	11	12	13	14	15	16
17	18	19	20	21	22	23
24	25	26	27	28	29	30

September

S	M	T	W	T	F	S
	1	2	3	4	5	6
7	8	9	10	11	12	13
14	15	16	17	18	19	20
21	22	23	24	25	26	27
28	29	30				

October

			1	2	3	4
5	6	7	8	9	10	11
12	13	14	15	16	17	18
19	20	21	22	23	24	25
26	27	28	29	30	31	

November

30						1
2	3	4	5	6	7	8
9	10	11	12	13	14	15
16	17	18	19	20	21	22
23	24	25	26	27	28	29

December

	1	2	3	4	5	6
7	8	9	10	11	12	13
14	15	16	17	18	19	20
21	22	23	24	25	26	27
28	29	30	31			

IMPORTANT DATES

January 2025

SUNDAY	MONDAY	TUESDAY	WEDNESDAY
			1 New Year's Day
5	6	7	8
12	13	14	15
19	20 Martin Luther King Day	21	22
26	27	28	29

THURSDAY	FRIDAY	SATURDAY
2	3	4
9	10	11
16	17	18
23	24	25
30	31	

NOTES

February 2025

SUNDAY	MONDAY	TUESDAY	WEDNESDAY
2	3	4	5
9	10	11	12
16	17 President's Day	18	19
23	24	25	26

THURSDAY	FRIDAY	SATURDAY
		1
6	7	8
13	14 Valentine's Day	15
20	21	22
27	28	

NOTES

March 2025

SUNDAY	MONDAY	TUESDAY	WEDNESDAY
30	31		
2	3	4	5
9	10	11	12
16	17 St. Patrick's Day	18	19
23	24	25	26

THURSDAY	FRIDAY	SATURDAY
		1
6	7	8
13	14	15
20	21	22
27	28	29

NOTES

April 2025

SUNDAY	MONDAY	TUESDAY	WEDNESDAY
		1	2
6	7	8	9
13	14	15	16
20 Easter	21	22	23
27	28	29	30

THURSDAY	FRIDAY	SATURDAY
3	4	5
10	11	12
17	18 Good Friday	19
24	25	26

NOTES

May 2025

SUNDAY	MONDAY	TUESDAY	WEDNESDAY
4	5	6	7
11 Mother's Day	12	13	14
18	19	20	21
25	26 Memorial Day	27	28

THURSDAY	FRIDAY	SATURDAY
1	2	3
8	9	10
15	16	17
22	23	24
29	30	31

NOTES

June 2025

SUNDAY	MONDAY	TUESDAY	WEDNESDAY
1	2	3	4
8	9	10	11
15 Father's Day	16	17	18
22	23	24	25
29	30		

THURSDAY	FRIDAY	SATURDAY
5	6	7
12	13	14
19	20	21
26	27	28

NOTES

July 2025

SUNDAY	MONDAY	TUESDAY	WEDNESDAY
		1	2
6	7	8	9
13	14	15	16
20	21	22	23
27	28	29	30

THURSDAY	FRIDAY	SATURDAY
3	4 Independence Day	5
10	11	12
17	18	19
24	25	26
31		

NOTES

August 2025

SUNDAY	MONDAY	TUESDAY	WEDNESDAY
31			
3	4	5	6
10	11	12	13
17	18	19	20
24	25	26	27

THURSDAY	FRIDAY	SATURDAY
	1	2
7	8	9
14	15	16
21	22	23
28	29	30

NOTES

September 2025

SUNDAY	MONDAY	TUESDAY	WEDNESDAY
	1 Labor Day	2	3
7	8	9	10
14	15	16	17
21	22	23	24
28	29	30	

THURSDAY	FRIDAY	SATURDAY
4	5	6
11	12	13
18	19	20
25	26	27

NOTES

October 2025

SUNDAY	MONDAY	TUESDAY	WEDNESDAY
			1
5	6	7	8
12	13 Columbus Day	14	15
19	20	21	22
26	27	28	29

THURSDAY	FRIDAY	SATURDAY
2	3	4
9	10	11
16	17	18
23	24	25
30	31 Halloween	

NOTES

November 2025

SUNDAY	MONDAY	TUESDAY	WEDNESDAY
30			
2	3	4	5
9	10	11 Veterans Day	12
16	17	18	19
23	24	25	26

THURSDAY	FRIDAY	SATURDAY
		1
6	7	8
13	14	15
20	21	22
27 Thanksgiving Day	28	29

NOTES

December 2025

SUNDAY	MONDAY	TUESDAY	WEDNESDAY
	1	2	3
7	8	9	10
14	15	16	17
21	22	23	24
28	29	30	31

THURSDAY	FRIDAY	SATURDAY
4	5	6
11	12	13
18	19	20
25 Christmas	26	27

NOTES

2026

January

S	M	T	W	T	F	S
				1	2	3
4	5	6	7	8	9	10
11	12	13	14	15	16	17
18	19	20	21	22	23	24
25	26	27	28	29	30	31

February

S	M	T	W	T	F	S
1	2	3	4	5	6	7
8	9	10	11	12	13	14
15	16	17	18	19	20	21
22	23	24	25	26	27	28

March

S	M	T	W	T	F	S
1	2	3	4	5	6	7
8	9	10	11	12	13	14
15	16	17	18	19	20	21
22	23	24	25	26	27	28
29	30	31				

April

S	M	T	W	T	F	S
			1	2	3	4
5	6	7	8	9	10	11
12	13	14	15	16	17	18
19	20	21	22	23	24	25
26	27	28	29	30		

May

S	M	T	W	T	F	S
31					1	2
3	4	5	6	7	8	9
10	11	12	13	14	15	16
17	18	19	20	21	22	23
24	25	26	27	28	29	30

June

S	M	T	W	T	F	S
	1	2	3	4	5	6
7	8	9	10	11	12	13
14	15	16	17	18	19	20
21	22	23	24	25	26	27
28	29	30				

IMPORTANT DATES

2026

July

S	M	T	W	T	F	S
			1	2	3	4
5	6	7	8	9	10	11
12	13	14	15	16	17	18
19	20	21	22	23	24	25
26	27	28	29	30	31	

August

S	M	T	W	T	F	S
30	31					1
2	3	4	5	6	7	8
9	10	11	12	13	14	15
16	17	18	19	20	21	22
23	24	25	26	27	28	29

September

S	M	T	W	T	F	S
		1	2	3	4	5
6	7	8	9	10	11	12
13	14	15	16	17	18	19
20	21	22	23	24	25	26
27	28	29	30			

October

S	M	T	W	T	F	S
				1	2	3
4	5	6	7	8	9	10
11	12	13	14	15	16	17
18	19	20	21	22	23	24
25	26	27	28	29	30	31

November

S	M	T	W	T	F	S
1	2	3	4	5	6	7
8	9	10	11	12	13	14
15	16	17	18	19	20	21
22	23	24	25	26	27	28
29	30					

December

S	M	T	W	T	F	S
		1	2	3	4	5
6	7	8	9	10	11	12
13	14	15	16	17	18	19
20	21	22	23	24	25	26
27	28	29	30	31		

IMPORTANT DATES

January 2026

SUNDAY	MONDAY	TUESDAY	WEDNESDAY
4	5	6	7
11	12	13	14
18	19 Martin Luther King Day	20	21
25	26	27	28

THURSDAY	FRIDAY	SATURDAY
1 New Year's Day	2	3
8	9	10
15	16	17
22	23	24
29	30	31

NOTES

February 2026

SUNDAY	MONDAY	TUESDAY	WEDNESDAY
1	2	3	4
8	9	10	11
15	16 President's Day	17	18
22	23	24	25

THURSDAY	FRIDAY	SATURDAY
5	6	7
12	13	14 Valentine's Day
19	20	21
26	27	28

NOTES

March 2026

SUNDAY	MONDAY	TUESDAY	WEDNESDAY
1	2	3	4
8	9	10	11
15	16	17 St. Patrick's Day	18
22	23	24	25
29	30	31	

THURSDAY	FRIDAY	SATURDAY
5	6	7
12	13	14
19	20	21
26	27	28

NOTES

April 2026

SUNDAY	MONDAY	TUESDAY	WEDNESDAY
			1
5 Easter	6 Easter Monday	7	8
12	13	14	15
19	20	21	22
26	27	28	29

THURSDAY	FRIDAY	SATURDAY
2	3	4
9	10	11
16	17	18
23	24	25
30		

NOTES

May 2026

SUNDAY	MONDAY	TUESDAY	WEDNESDAY
3	4	5	6
10 Mother's Day	11	12	13
17	18	19	20
24 / 31	25 Memorial Day	26	27

THURSDAY	FRIDAY	SATURDAY
	1	2
7	8	9
14	15	16
21	22	23
28	29	30

NOTES

June 2026

SUNDAY	MONDAY	TUESDAY	WEDNESDAY
	1	2	3
7	8	9	10
14	15	16	17
21 Father's Day	22	23	24
28	29	30	

THURSDAY	FRIDAY	SATURDAY
4	5	6
11	12	13
18	19	20
25	26	27

NOTES

July 2026

SUNDAY	MONDAY	TUESDAY	WEDNESDAY
			1
5	6	7	8
12	13	14	15
19	20	21	22
26	27	28	29

THURSDAY	FRIDAY	SATURDAY
2	3	4 Independence Day
9	10	11
16	17	18
23	24	25
30	31	

NOTES

August 2026

SUNDAY	MONDAY	TUESDAY	WEDNESDAY
2	3	4	5
9	10	11	12
16	17	18	19
23 / 30	24 / 31	25	26

THURSDAY	FRIDAY	SATURDAY
		1
6	7	8
13	14	15
20	21	22
27	28	29

NOTES

September 2026

SUNDAY	MONDAY	TUESDAY	WEDNESDAY
		1	2
6	7 Labor Day	8	9
13	14	15	16
20	21	22	23
27	28	29	30

THURSDAY	FRIDAY	SATURDAY
3	4	5
10	11	12
17	18	19
24	25	26

NOTES

October 2026

SUNDAY	MONDAY	TUESDAY	WEDNESDAY
4	5	6	7
11	12 Columbus Day	13	14
18	19	20	21
25	26	27	28

THURSDAY	FRIDAY	SATURDAY
1	2	3
8	9	10
15	16	17
22	23	24
29	30	31 Halloween

NOTES

November 2026

SUNDAY	MONDAY	TUESDAY	WEDNESDAY
1	2	3	4
8	9	10	11 Veterans Day
15	16	17	18
22	23	24	25
29	30		

THURSDAY	FRIDAY	SATURDAY
5	6	7
12	13	14
19	20	21
26 Thanksgiving Day	27	28

NOTES

December 2026

SUNDAY	MONDAY	TUESDAY	WEDNESDAY
		1	2
6	7	8	9
13	14	15	16
20	21	22	23
27	28	29	30

THURSDAY	FRIDAY	SATURDAY
3	4	5
10	11	12
17	18	19
24	25 Christmas	26
31		

NOTES

Notes

Notes

Notes

Notes

Made in the USA
Coppell, TX
19 May 2022

77919631R00079